I0393446

Mike Berg

Degenerate Work

‘

HcT! Press

Mike Berg   Degenerate Work

Design and introductory essay by SMoss

Mike Berg wishes to thank his metal work team,
İbrahim Togay, Mustafa Togay, Bekir Togay, Muhsin Öztürk
and for kilims
Burak Aydoğan and the weavers of Uşak

Please visit www.mikebergart.com

Works displayed in this book were included in an April 2017
exhibition at Site:Brooklyn, 167 7th St, Brooklyn NY, 11215

cover
Sparkling Armada of Promises 2
2017, gouache on page
31 x 23 cm

at right
Study for Ömer's Kilim
2016, gouache on paper
33.5 x 25 cm

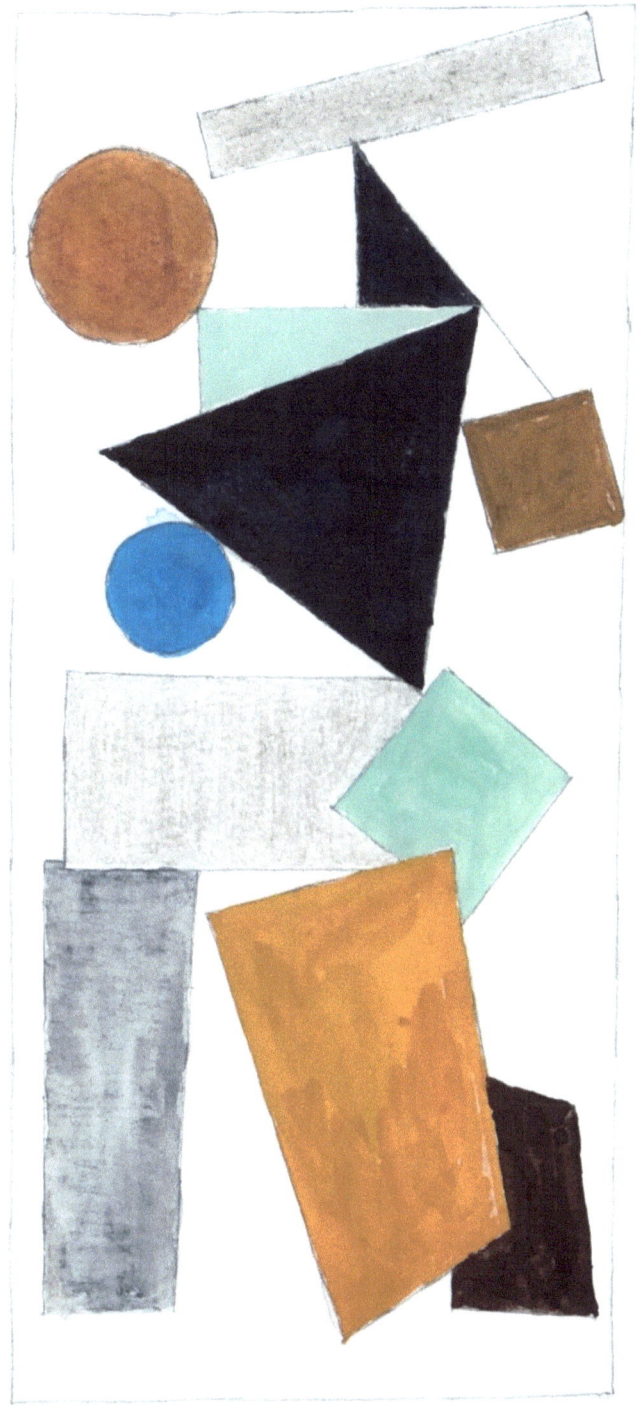

"All works degenerate over time." – Mike Berg

Who dares dispute that artistic creation is stable and static and endures the test of time? The essential presumption of permanence smacks of myth. Arrogance lends credibility to a work simply because of its survival? I'm sorry to disillusion you, but art is by nature ephemeral.

The cave paintings at Lascaux got lucky and were sealed for 20,000 years; as soon as people arrived on the scene the walls began to liquefy. The Neolithic settlement of Skara Brae lay buried under sand for 5000 years and was only revealed thanks to a hurricane; it will wash away in another 40 years. The occasional Etruscan helmet unearthed near Rome is never recovered in perfect condition. And the Hopi petroglyphs I saw on the reservation in Arizona were only there because they hadn't been ravaged by humans for the last seven centuries. Da Vinci's *Ultima Cena* deteriorated thanks to Leonardo's fiddling with the paint chemistry. Robert Smithson *Spiral Jetty* is settling into its lakebed, eventual disappearance a given. And don't get me started about *The Physical Impossibility of Death* by Damien Hirst or Basquiat's felt tip drawings on crumbling newsprint.

Mike Berg is correct: art inevitably succumbs to the simple vagaries of physics. Creation is followed by disintegration, then an ignominious particulate dispersal back into the impersonal universe. The physical properties of Mike Berg's prolific output reflect the semiotic statement that transformation forms a part of every work and thus every life. What tempers the superficiality of this realization is the unassailable fact that (forgive me if you've heard this before) all events have consequences. That is: every work we engage is imprisoned in time, subject to its constant erosion. Mike's work must be considered by factoring the intervention of history. Every drawing, every gouache, every weaving, every metal sculpture memorializes the spontaneity of creation in its gestures, symbolizes its transit through time, anticipates its destruction.

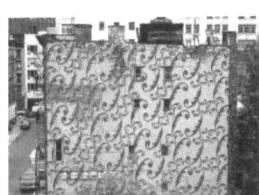

20 Renwick Wall Painting, NYC
1995, oil paint on facade
50 x 55'

Mike Berg was on to this idea as early as 1995. He painted a monumental mural on a wall at 20 Renwick Street. A repeat motif like the tick of a clock, overpainting an old billboard's faded remains. You saw it as you entered the Holland Tunnel, yet another metaphorical perspective on time and our unholy obsession with travel and conveyance in this impatient age. What is the mural's condition today? Degenerating. Repair has obscured it, but a subtle trace remains. Another 32 years and it will have turned to shadow, or be obliterated by the vision of a younger artist, if the structure survives.

Repetition figures, as these pages demonstrate. Of form, of material, of motif. Berg's hand has freed up, the counter-mechanical duplication which only the intervention of the human ergonomy can deliver. Calligraphic studies, color developments, iterations in iron, kilims and cicims- often produced in collaboration with traditional artisans- toy with the senses. But sensory engagement is – here comes that word again – ephemeral. We're compelled to experience these pieces in real time, studying their patina and surface, their pure physicality, ignoring the obvious: sooner than we like our fate will be the same as these luscious fabrications.

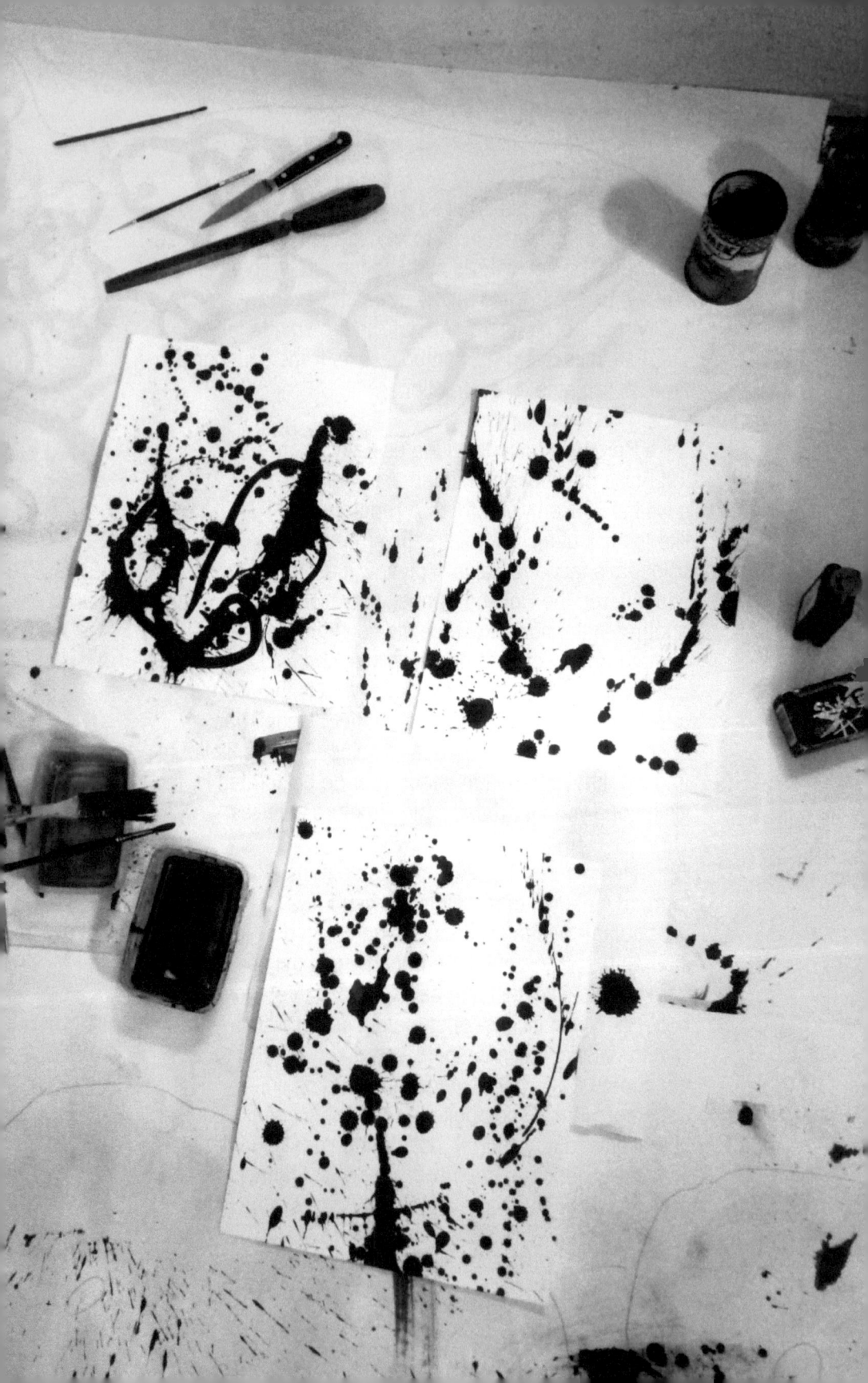

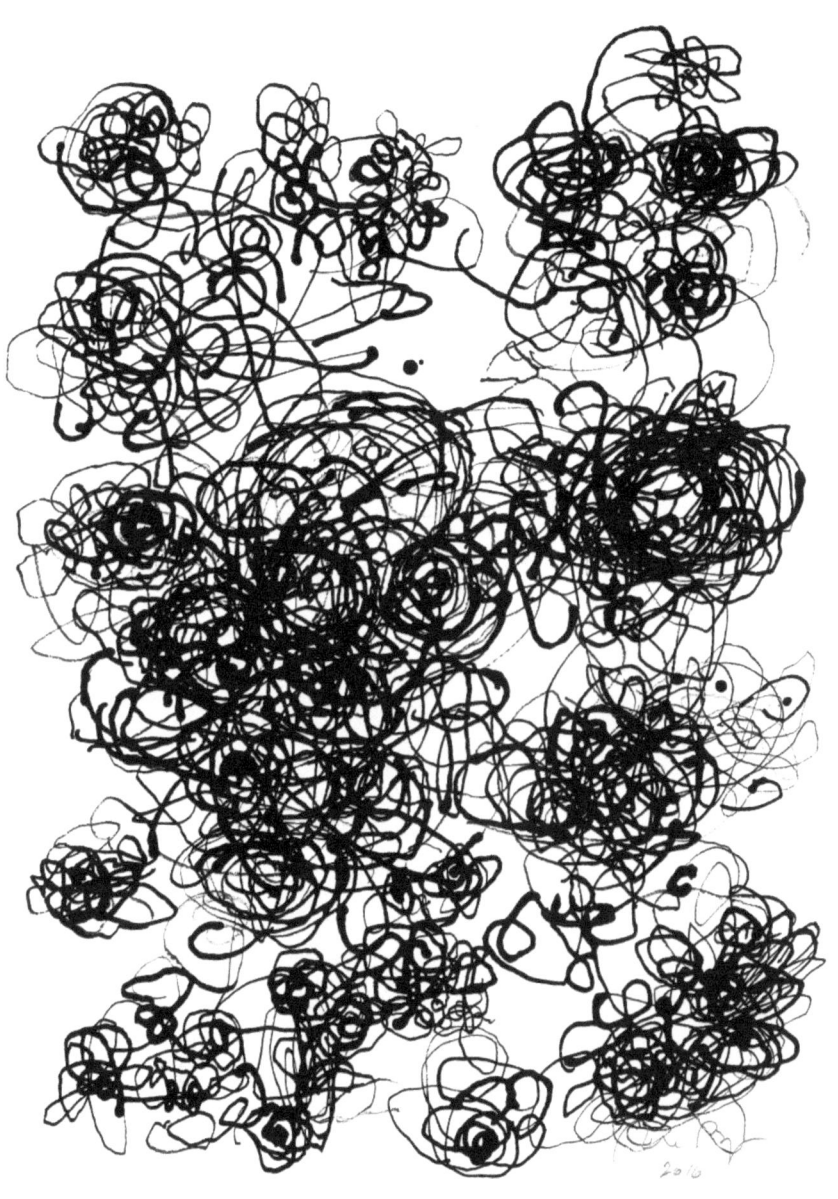

All the Lies I Never Told 7
2016, ink on paper
33.5 x 25cm

left
Istanbul Studio
2017, ink drawings in process

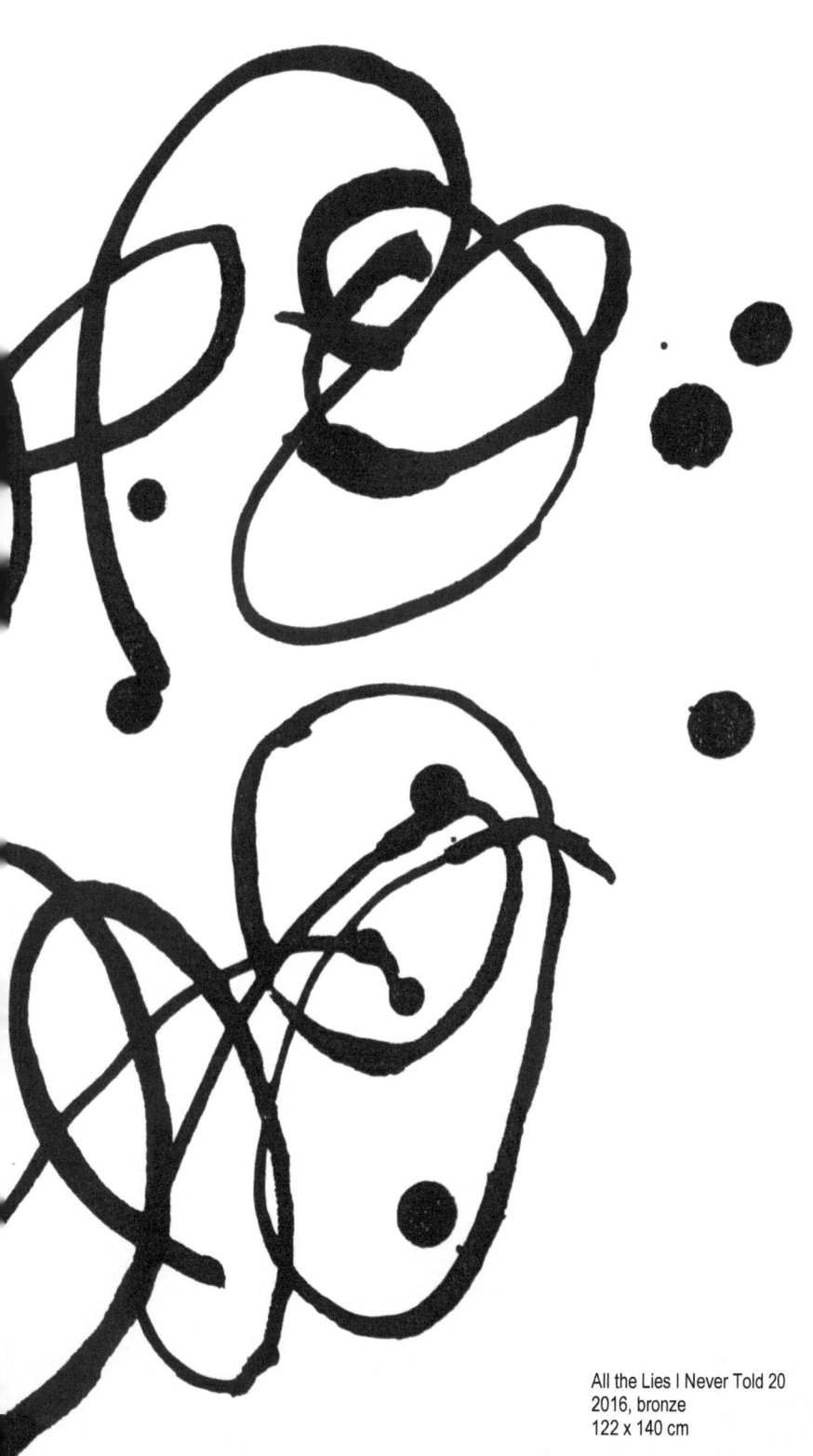

All the Lies I Never Told 20
2016, bronze
122 x 140 cm

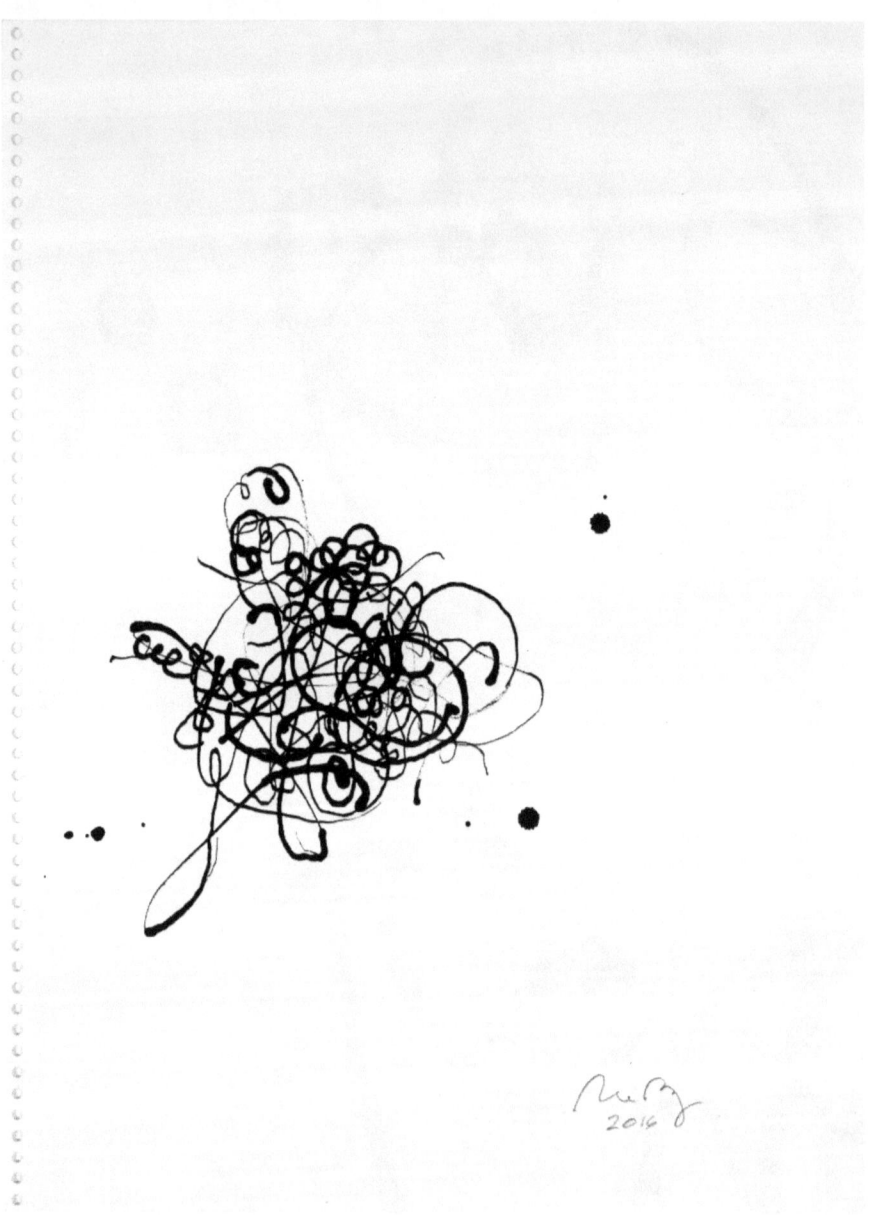

All the Lies I Never Told 7
2016, ink on paper
33.5 x 25cm

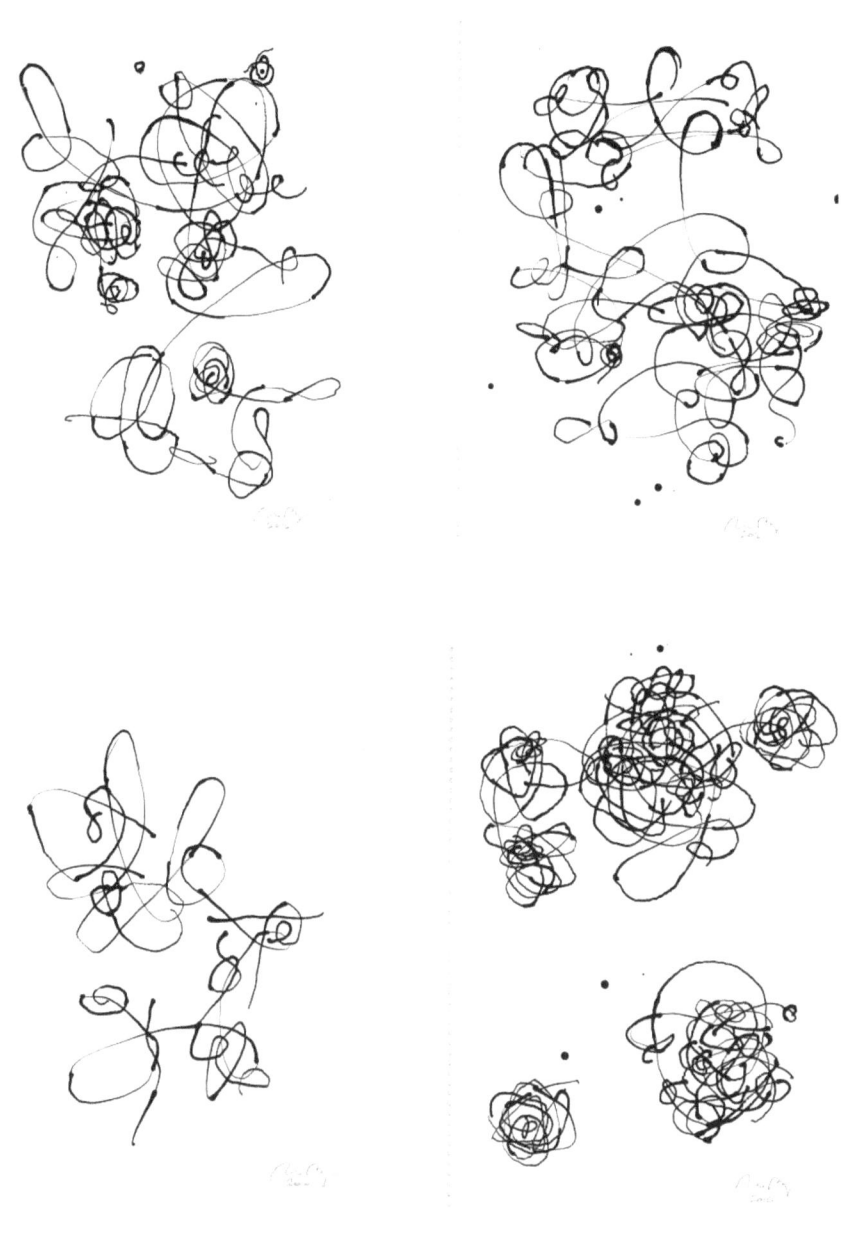

All the Lies I Never Told 9, *top left*
All the Lies I Never Told 11, *top right*
All the Lies I Never Told 10, *lower left*
All the Lies I Never Told 8, *lower right*
2016, ink on paper
33.5 x 25 cm

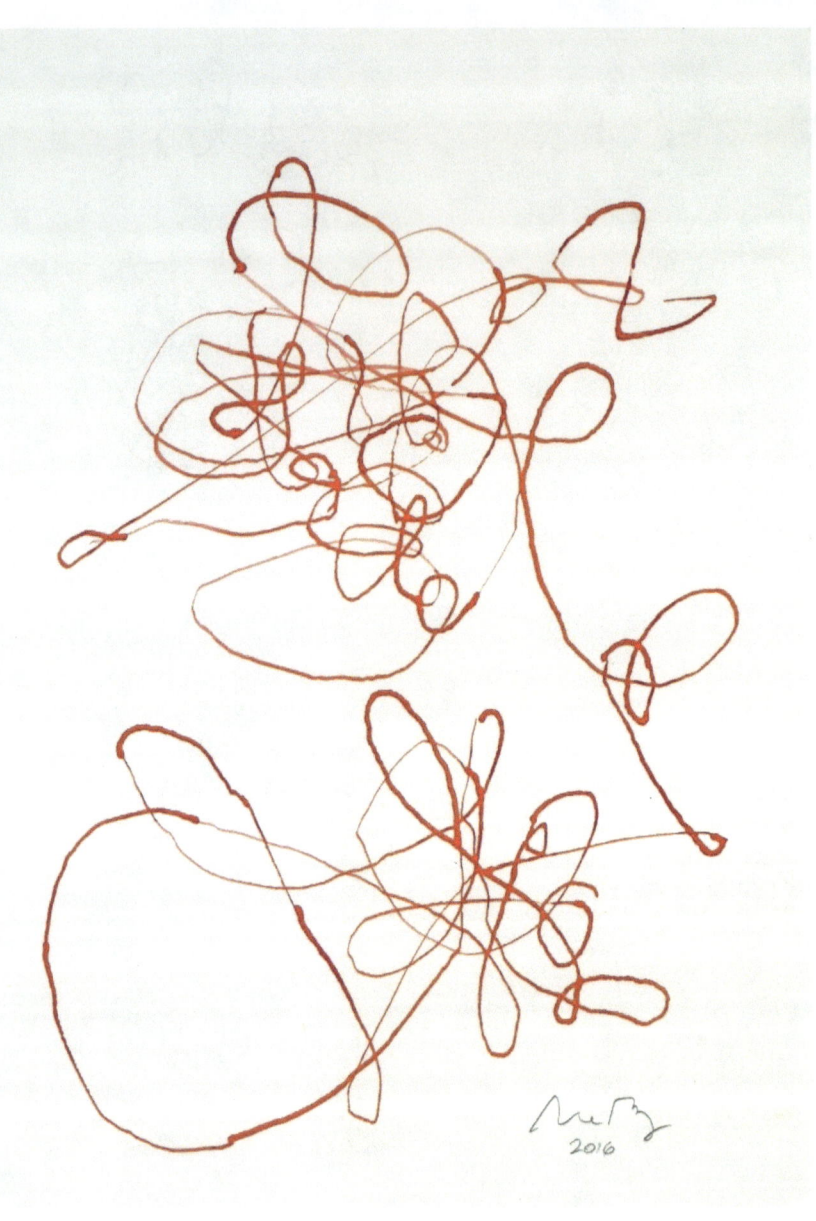

All the Lies I Never Told 5
2016, red ink on paper
33.5 x 25 cm

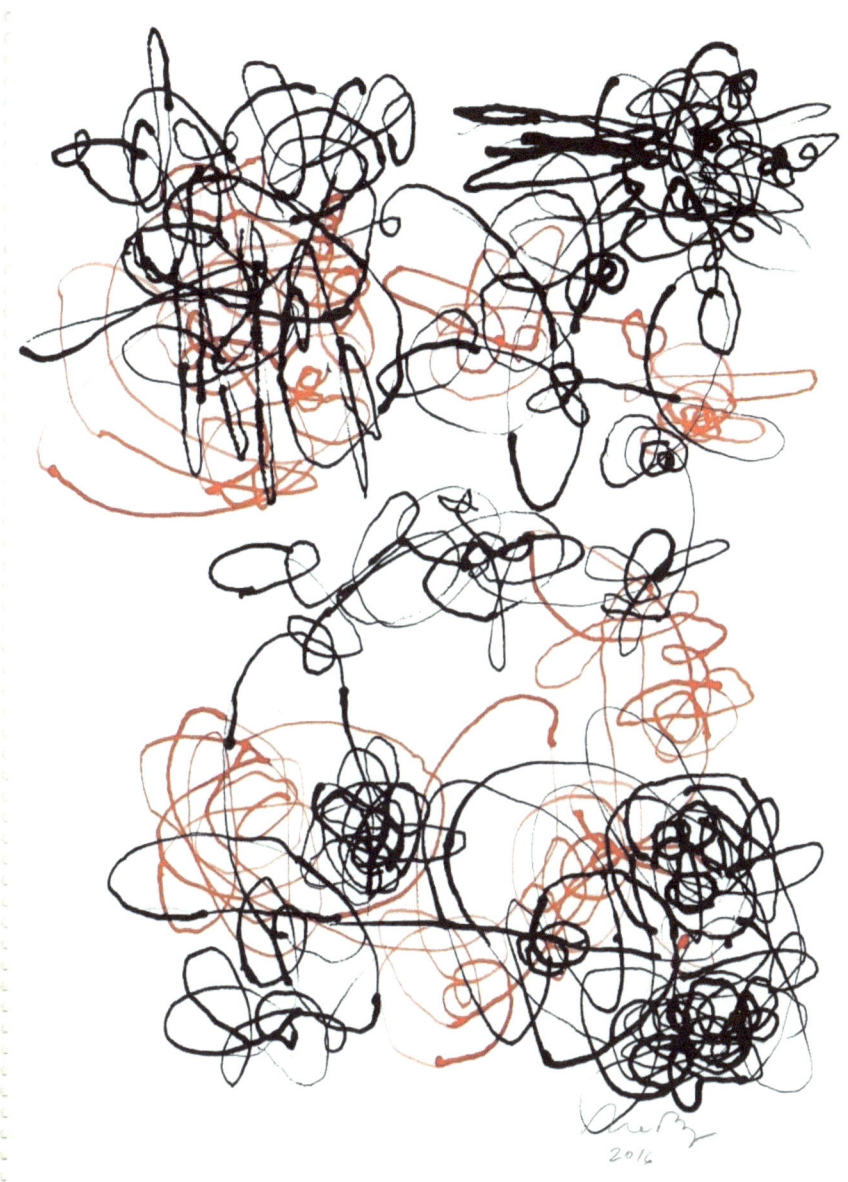

All the Lies I Never Told 4
2016, red and black ink on paper
33.5 x 25 cm

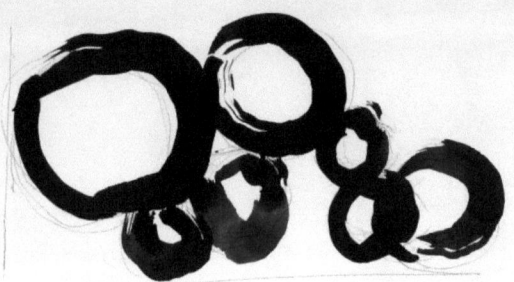

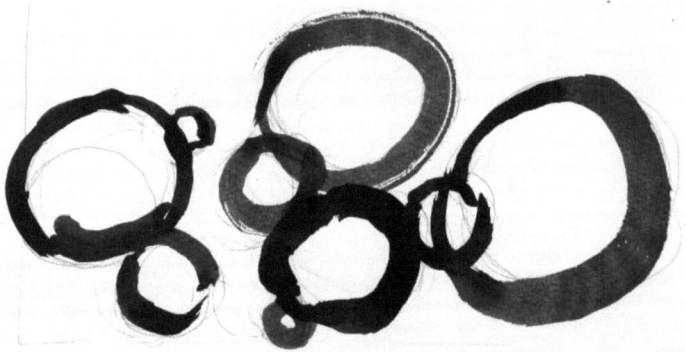

above
All the Lies I Never Told 3
2016, ink on paper
33.5 x 25 cm

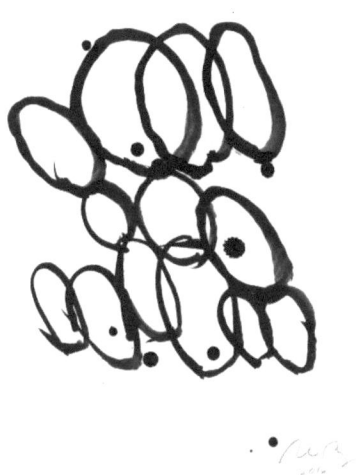
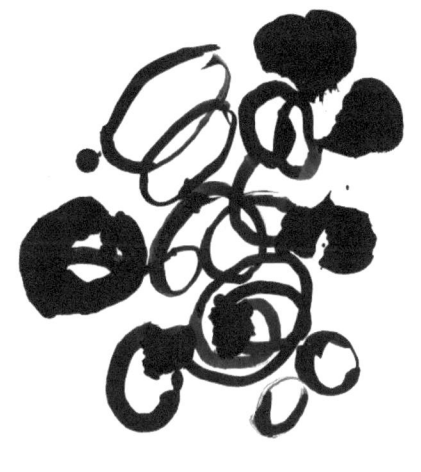
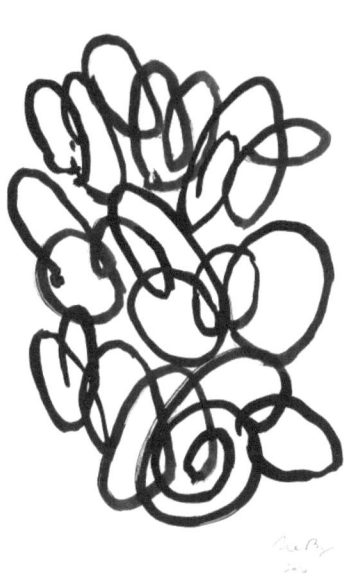
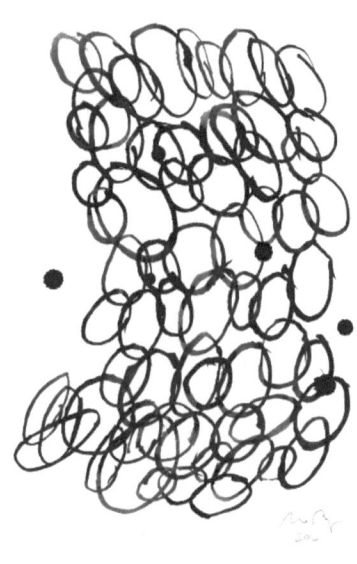

All the Lies I Never Told 19, *top left*
All the Lies I Never Told 17, *top right*
All the Lies I Never Told 16, *lower left*
All the Lies I Never Told 18, *lower right*
2016, ink on paper
35.5 x 27.5 cm

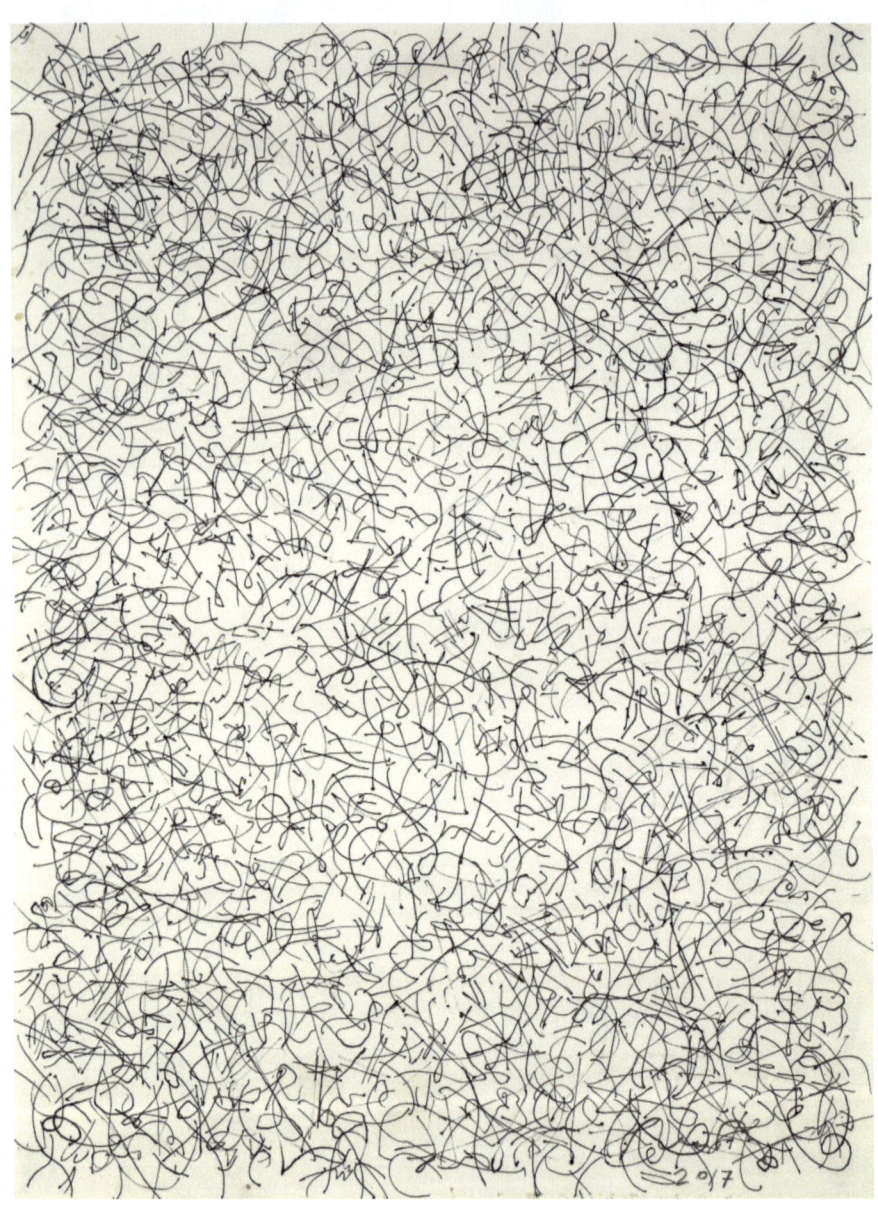

All the Lies I Never Told 1
2016, ink on paper
30 x 22.5 cm

right
Some Points and Edges 6,
2016, ink, pencil, gouache on paper
31 x 23 cm

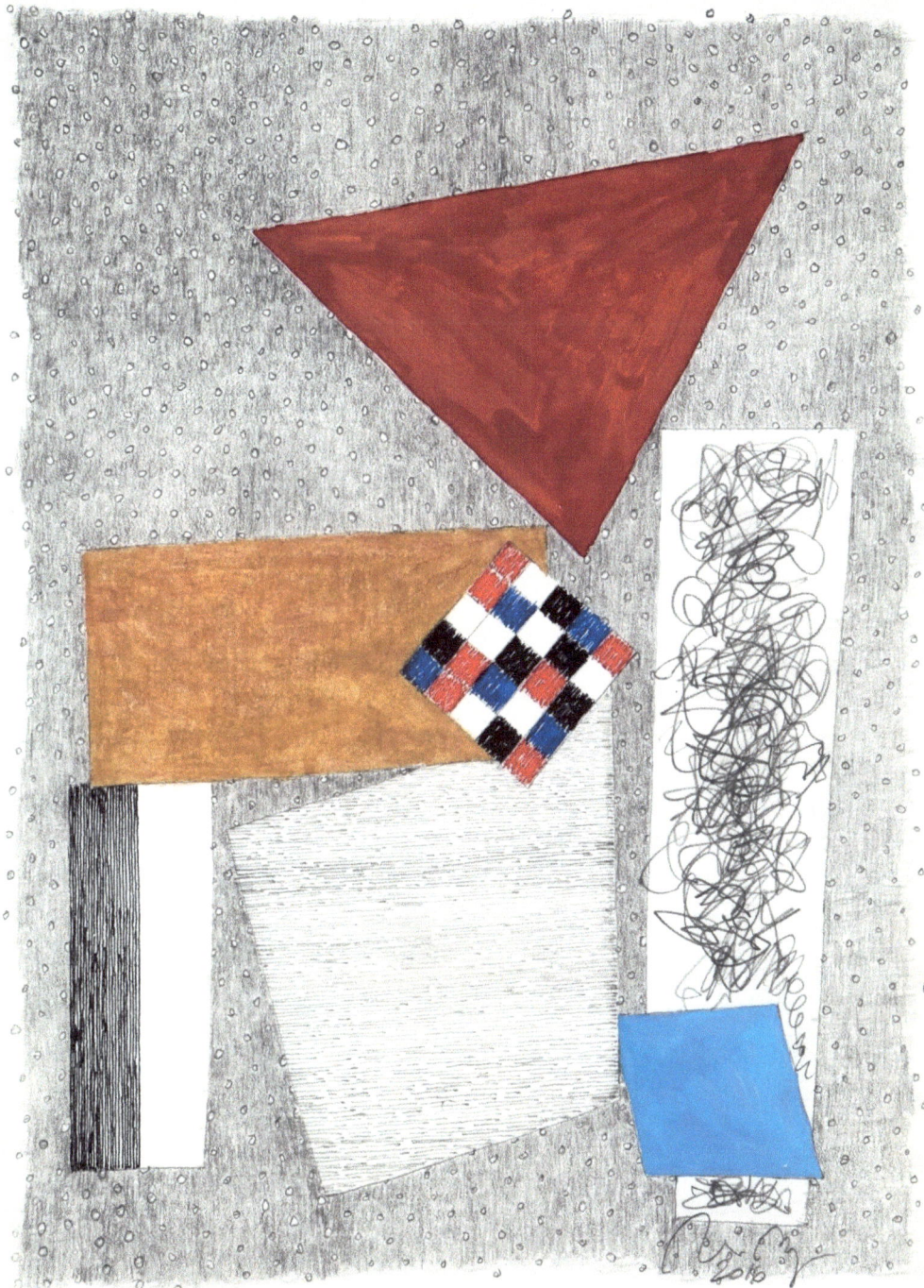

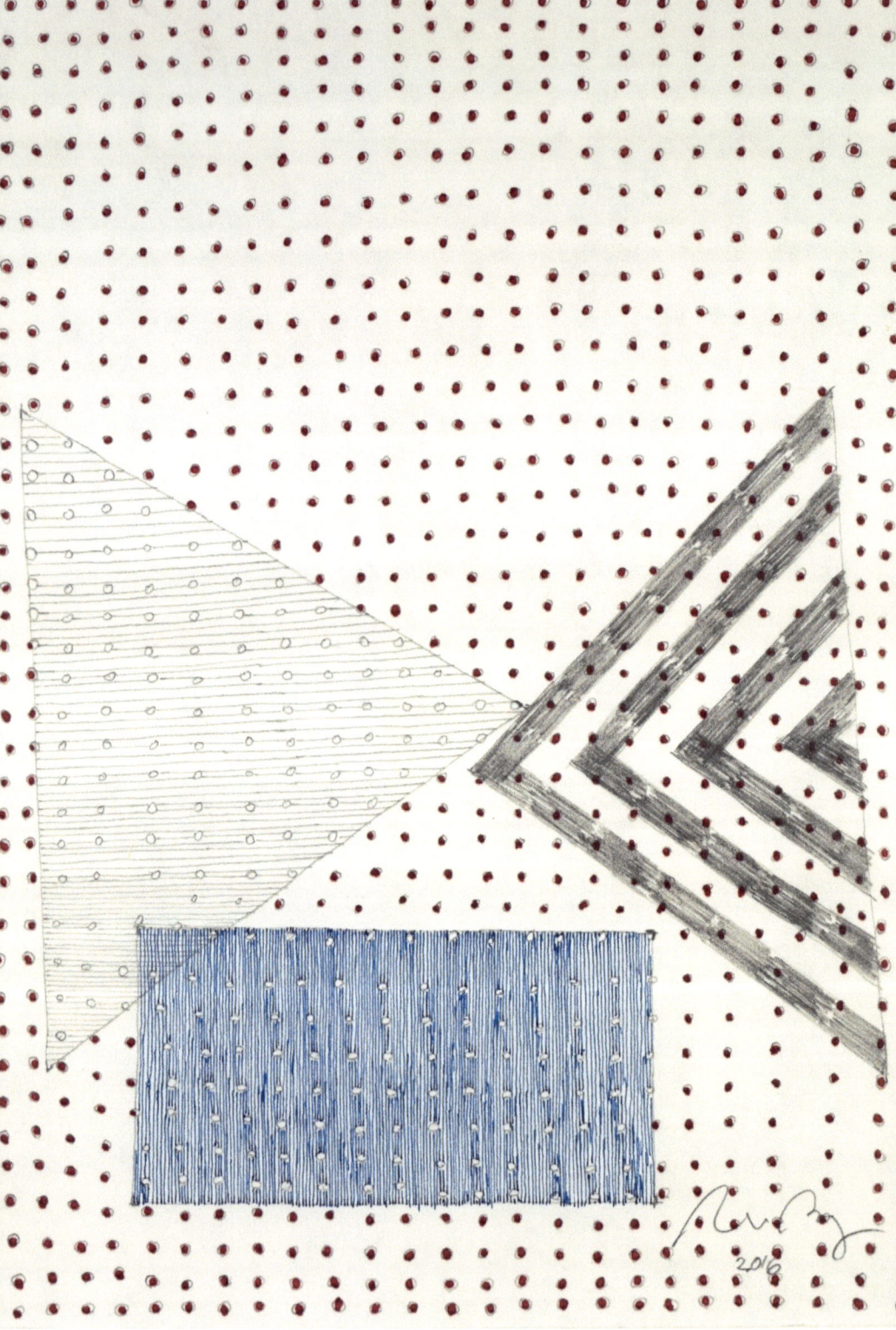

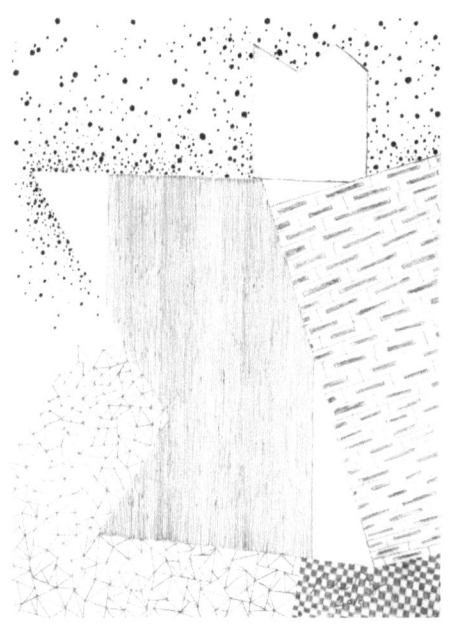

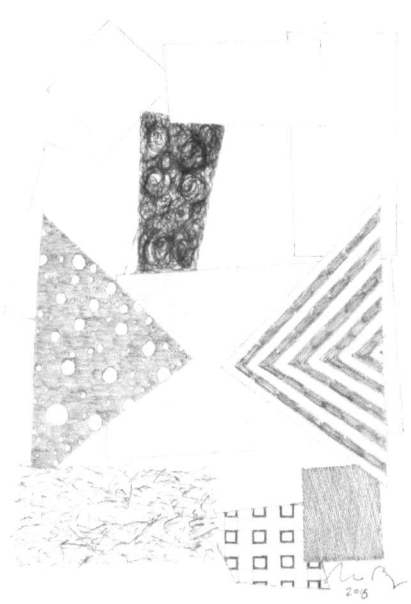

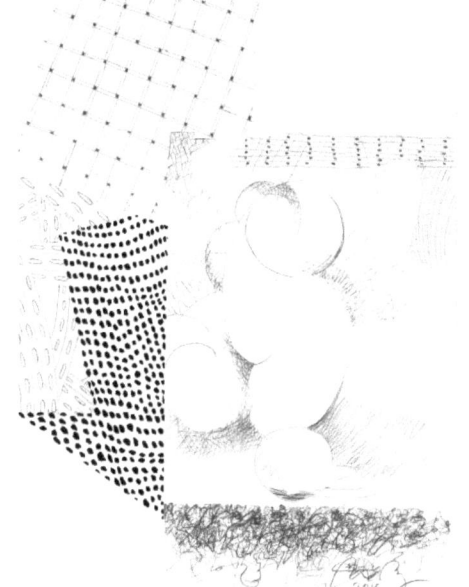

this page
Some Points and Edges 4, *top left*
2016, blue ink and pencil on paper
31 x 23 cm

Some Points and Edges 1, *top right*
2016, pencil on paper
31 x 23 cm

Some Points and Edges 7, *lower left*
2016, black ink and pencil on paper
31 x 23 cm

opposite left
Some Points and Edges 11
2016, red and blue ink on paper
31 x 23 cm

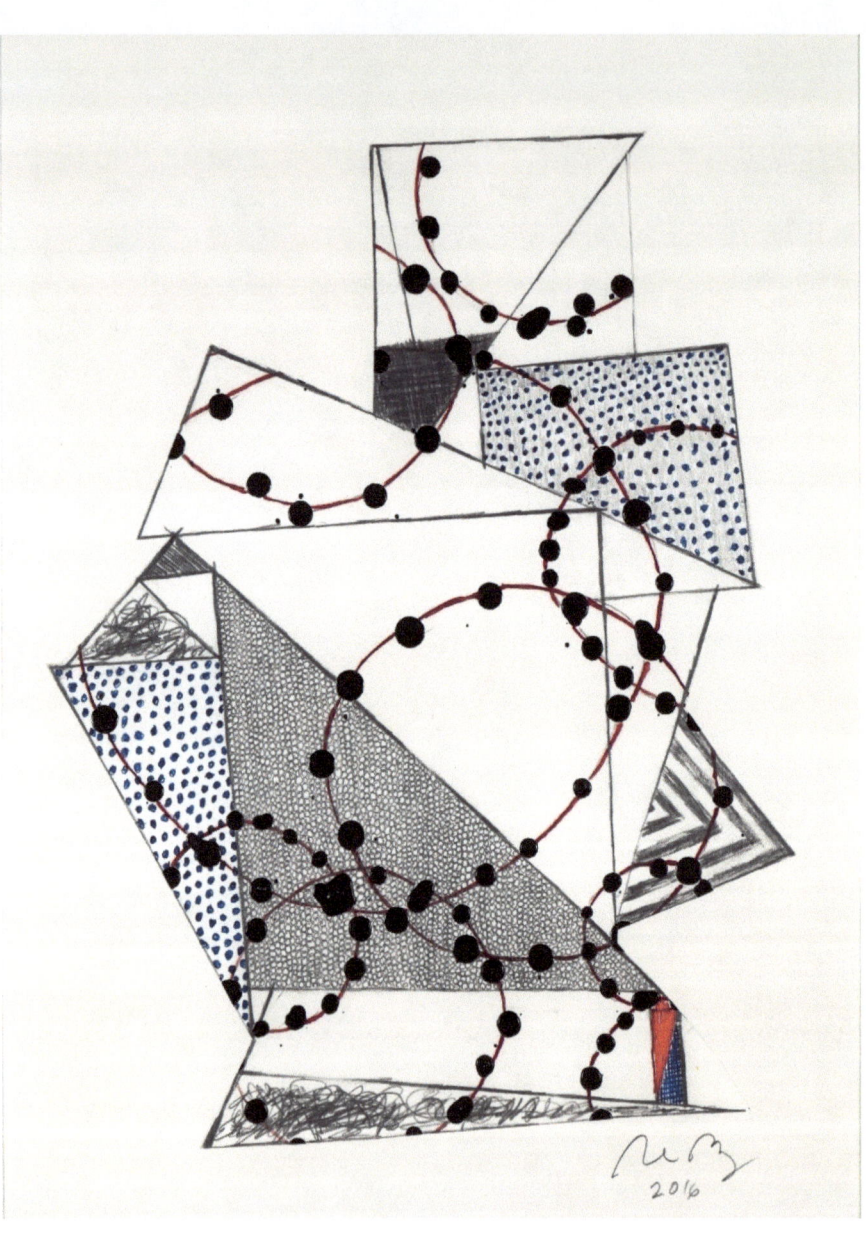

Some Points and Edges 2
2016, red and blue ink, black acrylic paint, pencil
31 x 23 cm

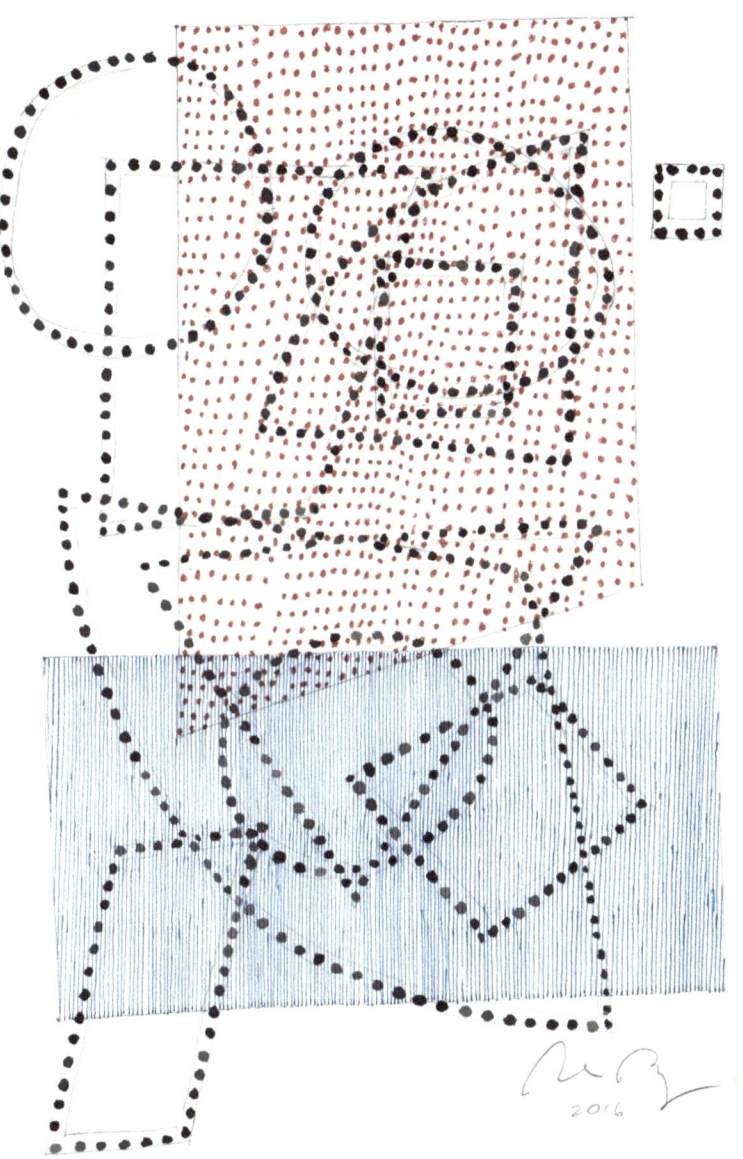

Some Points and Edges 9
2016, red and blue ink, acrylic paint, pencil
31 x 23 cm

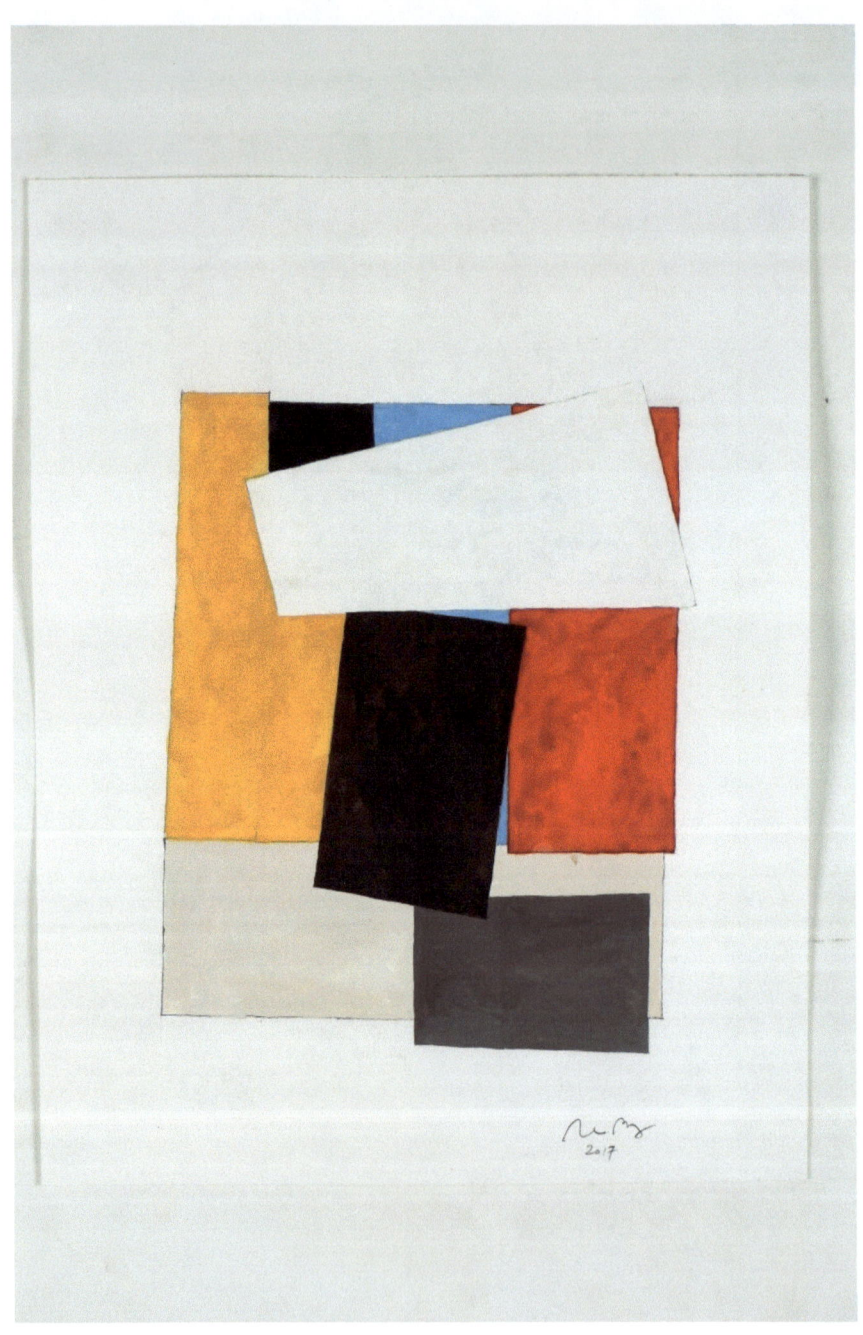

Sparkling Armada of Promises 9
2017, gouache on paper
35.5 x 27.5 cm

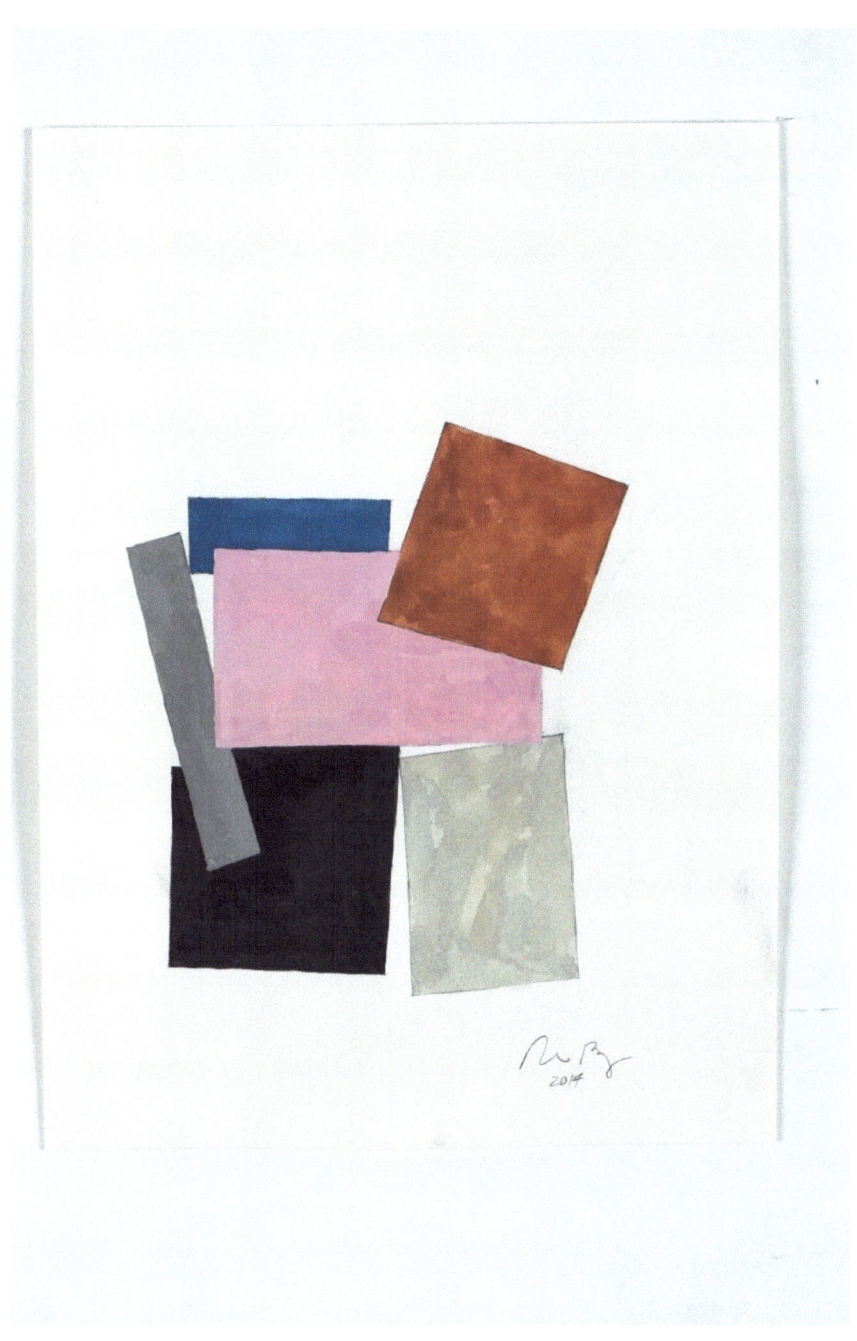

Sparkling Armada of Promises 4
2017, gouache on paper
31 x 23 cm

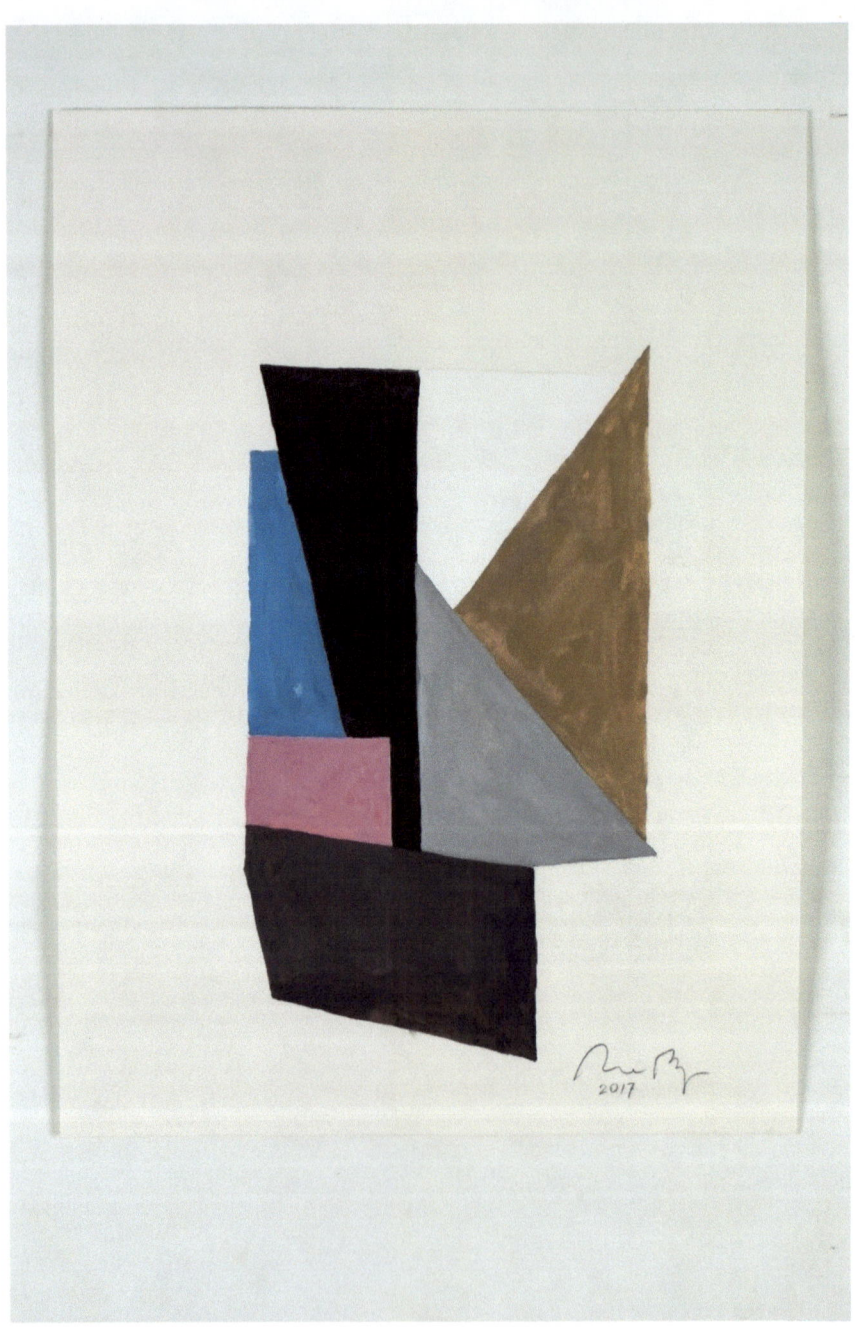

Sparkling Armada of Promises 5
2017, gouache on paper
31 x 23 cm
color study for Shape Shift, page 28

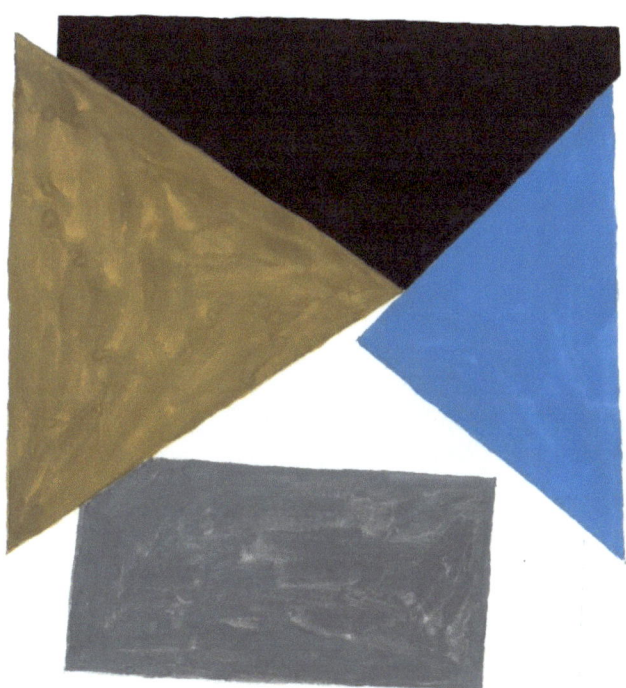

2017

Sparkling Armada of Promises 3
2017, gouache on paper
33.5 x 25 cm

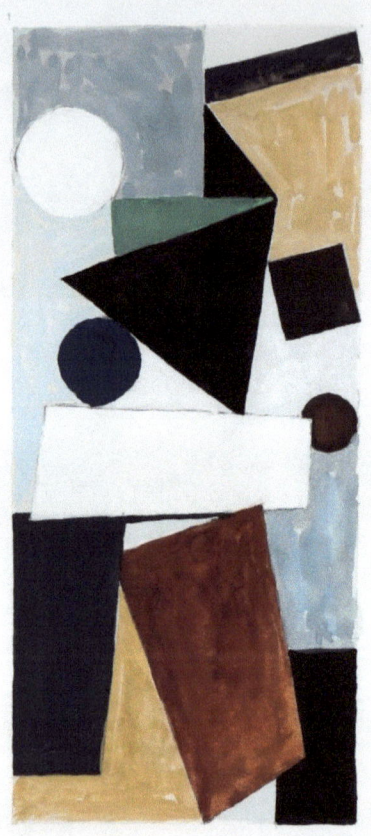

Emel Study 2
2016, gouache on paper
33.5 x 25 cm

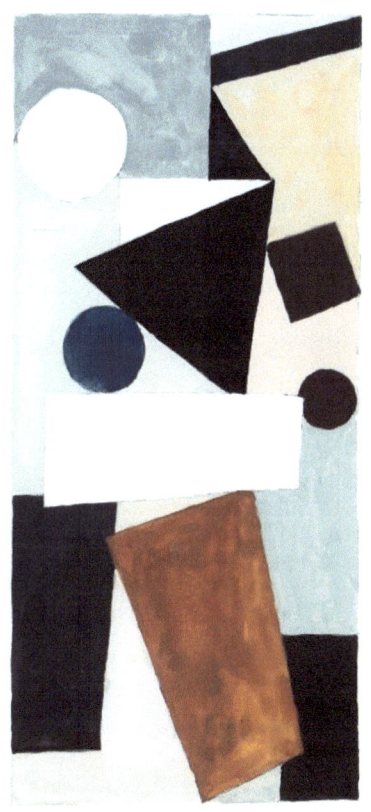

Emel Study 1
2016, gouache on paper
33.5 x 25 cm

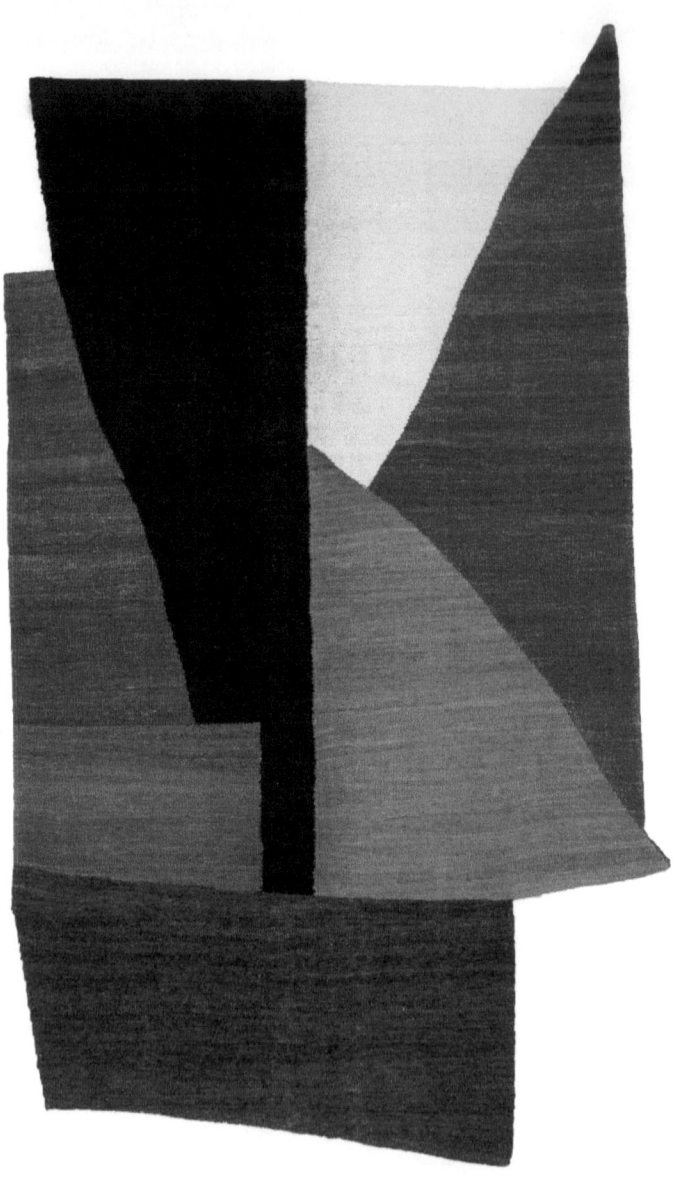

Shape Shift
2016, wool and cotton
191 x 99 cm
see color study, page 24

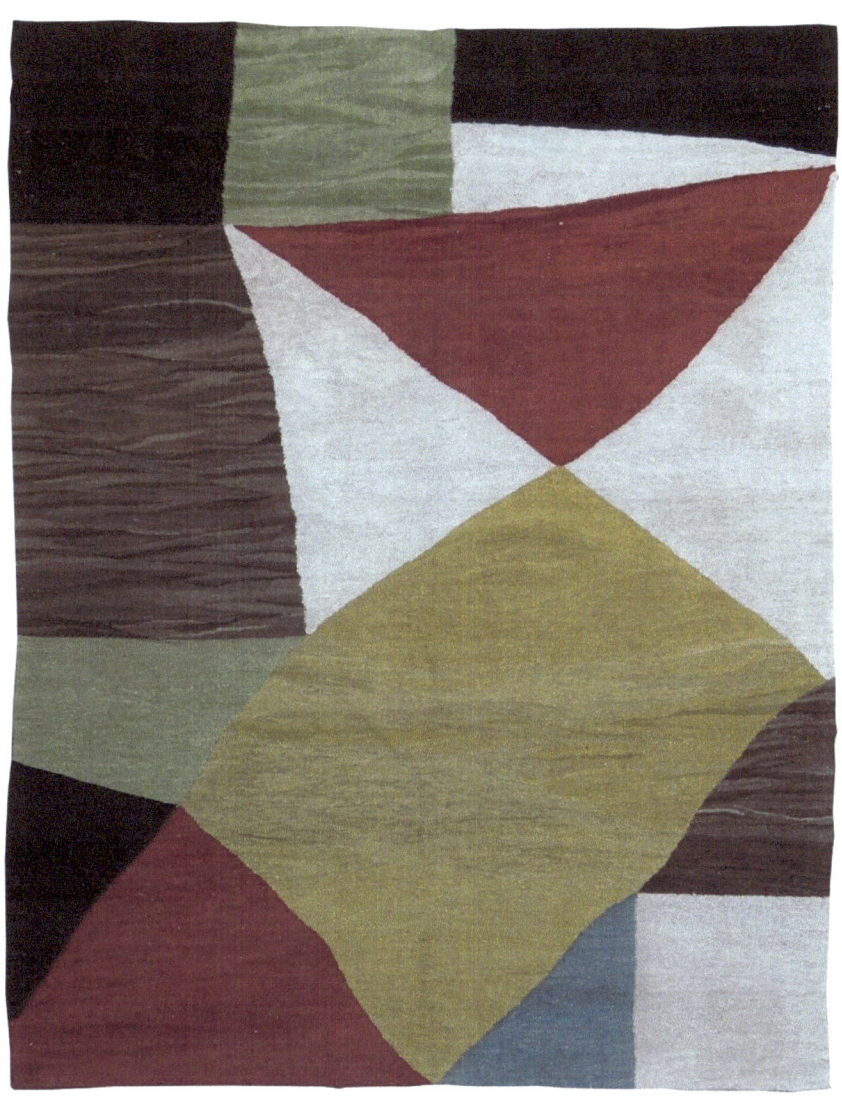

California Kilim
2011, wool, cotton and goat hair
250 x 185 cm

MIKE BERG

b. 1948 Portland, Oregon USA
Lives and works in Istanbul, Turkey and New York, NY

EDUCATION
1971 BA University of Washington, Seattle
1972 BFA, Fort Wright College, Spokane, WA
1972 Resident, Skowhegan School of Painting and Sculpture, MA

SOLO EXHIBITIONS
2017 Degenerate Work, Site: Brooklyn , NY.
2016 The Stremmel Gallery, Reno, Nevada
2015 Kocaman Kafes, at Galeri Nev, Istanbul, Turkey
2013-14 Recent Textiles, Museum of Contemporary Art, San Diego
2013 Mike Berg: Taking Chances, Museum of Contemporary Art, San Diego
2012 Simple Geometry, Galeri Nev, Istanbul, Turkey
2012 Believing in Impossible Things, Ankara, Turkey
2011 5/3 Insane, PGArtSpace, Istanbul, Turkey
2010 Heavy Metal, Galeri Nev, Istanbul, Turkey
2008 The Aftermath of Sunny Days, Galeri Nev, Istanbul, Turkey
2006 Run My Hand Around The Font, Center for Contemporary Art, Seattle, WA
You Can't Say It That Way Anymore, Galeri Nev, Istanbul, Turkey
2005 Galleons And Towers, Kadir Has Üniversitesi, Istanbul, Turkey
2004 Mistaking Street Lamps for Planets, Lorinda Knight Gallery, Spokane, WA
2003 Mike Berg at the Hagia Sofia Museum, Istanbul, Turkey
Bronze Age, Galeri Nev, Istanbul, Turkey
2001 Florence DeVoldere Salon, Paris, France
2000 Little House of Our Desire, Dulcinea, Istanbul, Turkey
What Days Are For, Sling Shot Gallery, New York, NY
What Days Are For, Heriard/Cimino Gallery, New Orleans, LA
1999 Now It Goes Smoothly, Gina Fiore Salon of Fine Arts, Chelsea Hotel, New York, NY
Now It Goes Smoothly, Eastern Washington University, Cheney, WA
1998 A Family of Stories, Boulder Museum of Contemporary Art, Boulder, CO
1997 A Haven of Serenity and Unreachable, Rule Gallery, Denver, CO
Patterns in Time, Maria Henle Studio, St. Croix, USVI
1995 Visions Fugitives, Elaine Kaufman Cultural Center, New York, NY
A History of Backward Glances, Lee Arthur Studio, New York, NY
1993 Lee Arthur Studio, New York, NY
1991 Sharon Truax Gallery, Venice, CA
1990 McGrath Gallery, Los Angeles, CA

1989 56 Bleecker Gallery, New York, NY
1989 Earl McGrath Gallery, Los Angeles, CA
1987 Inaugural Exhibition, The Queens Museum, New York, NY
The Donald Wren Gallery, New York, NY
Interior/Exterior: Architectural Fantasies, Untitled, The Queens Museum,
New York, NY
1986 Guid'Arte Gallery, Rome, Italy
1985 Louisiana State University, School of Art Gallery, Baton Rouge
1984 Noel Butcher Gallery, Philadelphia, PA

COMMISSIONS
1998 Mural Project: The Days Now Move From Left to Right, Boulder Museum
of Contemporary Art, CO
1998 Mural Project: A Walk Across Continents, Christopher and Alida Latham,
Seattle, WA
1995 Mural Project: 20 Renwick Street, New York, NY

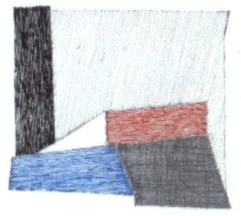

Sparkling Armada of Promises 1
2016, red, black and blue ink, pencil on paper
33.5 x 25 cm

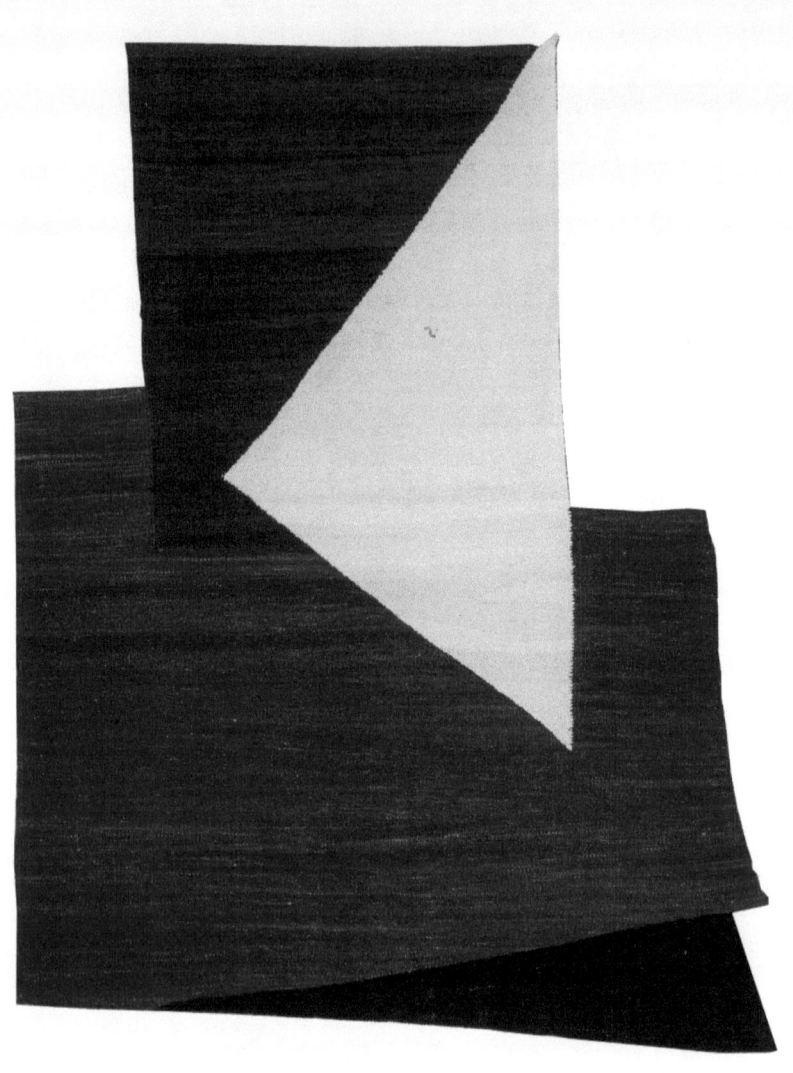

Shapes and Shingles
2016, wool and cotton
169 x 129 cm

ENJOY THESE OTHER TITLES FROM 'HcT! PRESS

111 Haikus

2014 Global Brand Letter
2015 Global Brand Letter

24 Poems *by Marco Fazzini*

Blindés *by Alexandre d'Huy*

The Blue Tibetan Poppy

The Book of Deals

Case Studies
of Five Modern Labyrinths

The Captain Blackpool Trilogy
The Crimson Garter
Fate & the Pearls

Classic: *A Love Letter
to Milo Reice*

DO NOT *– a book of rules*

The Grandpa Trio
Grandpa Goes Shopping
Grandpa Does Yoga
Grandpa Takes A Walk

The History & Adventures
of the Bandit Joaquin Murietta

Hammam Ladies

Hitman in Delhi, *a screenplay*

La Toux *by Pierre d'Huy*

Leaving Your Dragon

Legacy & Power

Mandalas *by Cat Soubbotnik*

Marrakech: *A Friendly Travel
Guide to The Medina*

Oasis: *A Love Letter
to Rancho Dulce*

Park Avenue Poop

Paula's Proverbs, Volume I
Paula's Proverbs, Volume II

Return to Paradise:
A Love Letter to Catalina

Riding the Storm *by Marco Fazzini*

Supari

Supernatural

Surf City: *A Love Letter
to Santa Teresa*

Swami Gopal Buri

Time Out For Dragon!

VSB

The Vicentini

What Is A Brand?

www.ingramcontent.com/pod-product-compliance
Lightning Source LLC
Chambersburg PA
CBHW041133200526
45172CB00018B/309